Knitting

by MAUREEN and MICHAEL HARVEY

with illustrations by
ERIC WINTER

Publishers: Ladybird Books Ltd . Loughborough
© Ladybird Books Ltd (formerly Wills & Hepworth Ltd) 1972
Printed in England

Do's and don'ts for better knitting

Before you start knitting, there are some important things to remember. These are:

1. Always wash your hands before you begin to knit— dirty hands make dirty work!

2. Make sure you use the size knitting needles given in the instructions you are following.

3. Count the stitches on your needles every now and again in case you accidentally lose some.

4. Never leave your knitting halfway through a row.

5. Do not push your knitting needles through your ball of wool, as this may split the wool.

0 7214 0310 7

The things you will need

For your knitting, you will need:

A pair of children's size 8 KNITTING NEEDLES.

These should not have sharp points.

Lots of little balls of brightly coloured, DOUBLE KNITTING WOOL with which you can practise.

A small pair of SCISSORS for cutting the wool.

A WOOL SEWING NEEDLE which has a big eye.

It is useful (though not essential at this early stage) to have some sort of TIDY-BAG in which to keep all the things needed for your knitting. It will also help to keep your work clean.

How to begin

First of all you have to make a slip loop. This is a loop that slips so that it can be pulled tight.

Making a Slip Loop

Use a ball of brightly coloured double knitting wool. Make a loop with your fingers just like the loop shown in the illustration (Picture 1).

Then loop some more of the wool through this first loop to make another loop (Picture 2).

Put the new loop you have made onto one of your knitting needles. Then pull this loop tight (but not too tight) so that the knot comes under the needle (Picture 3).

Now that you have made a loop, put the needle which has the loop on it in your left hand. This will be your first cast on stitch.

You will have to make some more loops before you can start knitting, but these will have to be made in a different way.

Making these other loops is called CASTING ON.

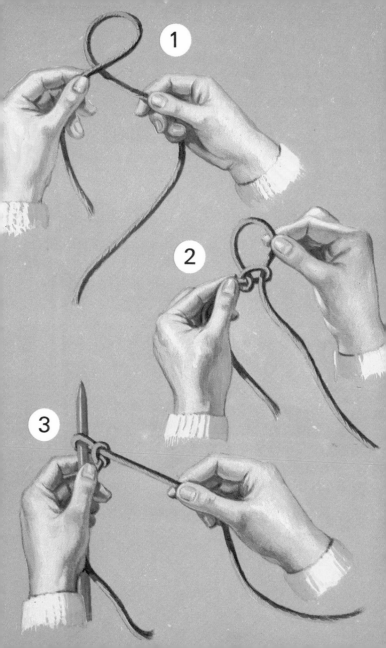

Casting on

Pick up the empty needle in your right hand.

Push the point of this empty needle into the front of the loop on the other needle, making sure that the empty needle goes under the other one (Picture 1). Then wind the wool round the needle in your right hand (Picture 2).

Now pull the wool through the loop with the under needle. This makes a new loop (Picture 3).

Put this new loop onto the needle you are holding in your left hand so that you have two loops on that needle. The needle in your right hand will be empty again.

Then make some more loops in the same way. Each time you make a loop on the needle you are holding in your right hand, you must put this onto the left-hand needle.

The number of loops on the left-hand needle will grow and grow, while the needle in your right hand will stay empty.

When you start your work like this, it is called CASTING ON.

The illustration shows a needle after thirteen loops have been made on it.

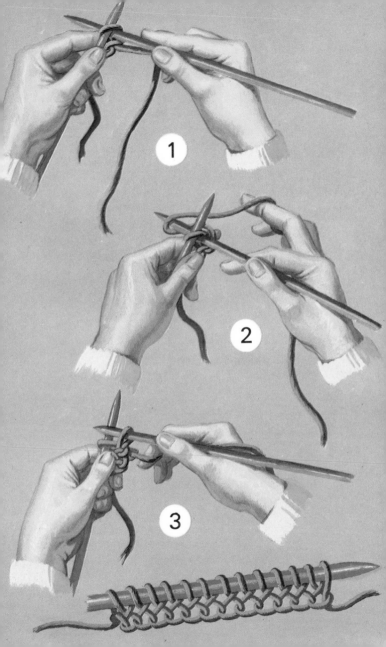

Making a row of plain knitting

Now that you have learned how to cast on, you can learn how to make plain stitches. All the cast-on loops you have made should be on the needle you are holding in your left hand, while the needle in your right hand should be empty.

Now push the point of the empty needle into the front of the first cast-on loop on the left-hand needle (Picture 1).

Wind the wool round the needle in your right hand (Picture 2).

Now pull the wool you have wound round the right-hand needle, through the loop on the needle in your left hand (Picture 3).

When you have done this, you will have made your first knitted stitch. Leave this stitch on the needle you are holding in your right hand and slip the loop, into which you have pushed this needle, from the left-hand needle (Picture 4). Do the same with each loop on the left-hand needle until you have made new stitches for all the loops on this needle.

As you go along the row making the new stitches, the right-hand needle gets more and more stitches on it, while the one in your left hand has fewer and fewer stitches until there are no more left.

When you have finished all the stitches, you will have made your very first row of knitting.

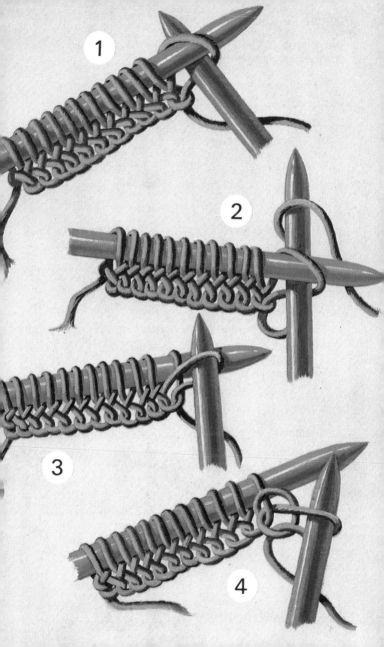

Knitting plain stitches every row makes garter stitch

When you have finished making your first row of knitting, you will find that all the new stitches are on the needle held in your right hand, while the one in your left hand is empty.

Now you must change the needles over into opposite hands, and you MUST do this every time you need to start a new row.

You are now ready to make a second row of knitting. Do this in just the same way as you made the first. (If you cannot remember how to do this, go back and read page 12.)

After you have made your second row of knitting you can make another, and another, and another, until you have as many rows as you wish.

When you make plain stitches, this is called making the KNIT STITCH. When you make knit stitches every row, it is called GARTER STITCH.

When you make garter stitch the work looks like a lot of ridges, and you will see that the knitting looks the same on both sides.

How to finish

When you have made enough rows in the plain stitch, say twenty rows for practice, you must end your piece of work. This is called CASTING OFF.

To do this, hold the needle with all the stitches on in your left hand, and hold the empty needle in your right hand—exactly as you do when starting a new row of plain knitting.

Knit the first two stitches as you did before. Now you have two stitches on the right-hand needle (Picture 1).

Slip the point of the needle you are holding in your left hand into the first stitch you knitted on the other needle (Picture 2). This stitch is then pulled over the second one you made and right off the right-hand needle. When you have done this, you will have made two stitches into one (Picture 3).

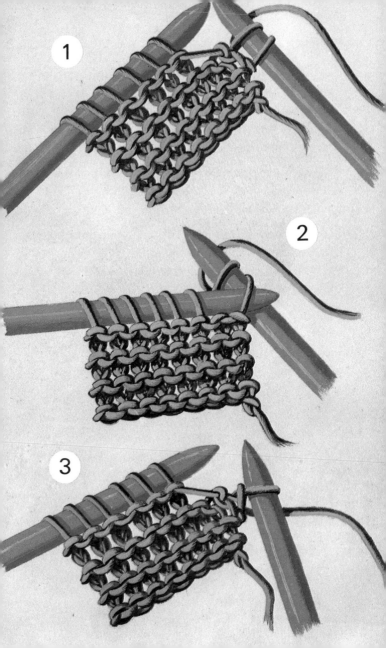

Casting off some more stitches

After you have cast off one stitch you must do the same with the other stitches. So knit two stitches into one all along the row. (If you cannot remember how to make two stitches into one, go back again to page 16 where you can read how to do this.)

Keep on making two stitches into one. As you do this, you will find there are fewer and fewer stitches on the needle you are holding in your left hand.

When there are no more stitches remaining on the left-hand needle and only one on the right-hand needle, get your scissors from the 'tidy-bag' and cut the wool 4 inches from your work.

Then pull the end of the wool through the stitch which remains on the right-hand needle (the picture shows you how to do this). Now draw this loose end of wool tight and slip your last stitch off the needle.

When you have done this, you will have finished your first piece of knitting.

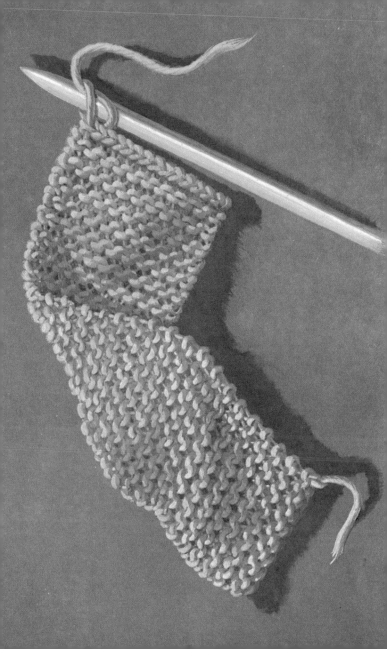

Something to knit—a hair-band

By now you will have learned how to make plain stitches. You can also start some knitting and finish it off. Now you can knit something useful.

If you wish you can make a hair-band. This will help you to practise knitting.

You will need some double knitting wool in a bright colour. Using size 8 needles, cast on eight stitches.

Now make garter stitch (see page 14), and keep on knitting this until you have a piece of work almost long enough to fit your head. Then cast off.

When you have finished the knitting, you will have to ask Mother for a piece of elastic to join the ends of the hair-band so that it fits comfortably.

Having now made something useful, you will want to learn more about knitting.

Making the purl stitch

You have learned how to make the plain stitch, so now you can learn how to make the purl stitch.

Cast on loops in the same way as you did before (page 10). Then make one row of plain stitches. When you have done this, change the needles into opposite hands so that the one which had all the stitches on is in your left hand and the empty one is in your right hand. Now you are ready to make PURL STITCHES.

Put the empty needle through the first stitch on the left-hand needle BUT this time do it from behind (Picture 1).

Wind the wool round the needle in your right hand to make a loop (Picture 2).

Pull this loop through the stitch on the left-hand needle (Picture 3).

Now leave this new stitch on the needle in your right hand while you slip off the loop from the left-hand needle (Picture 4). When you have done this, you will have made your first purl stitch.

Now you must do the same for all the other stitches on the left-hand needle. You will then have made a row of purl knitting.

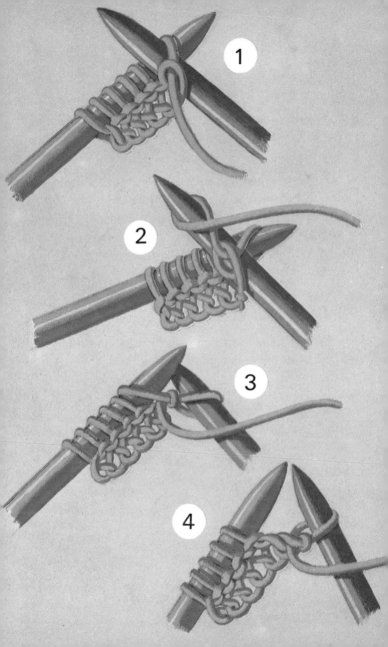

Stocking stitch

A row of plain stitches, followed by a row of purl stitches makes STOCKING STITCH.

You have just learned how to do purl knitting, and know how to do plain knitting, so you can now learn how to knit STOCKING STITCH.

To make stocking stitch, a row of purl knitting must always be followed by a row of plain knitting, so after you have finished your row of purl knitting, knit a row of plain stitches. Then carry on making one row of purl knitting, followed by one row of plain knitting for a few rows.

You will find that when you make stocking stitch, one side of your work looks different from the other.

Picture 1 shows the right side of stocking stitch. This is the side that looks smooth.

Picture 2 shows the wrong side of stocking stitch. This side has lots of ridges and looks rough.

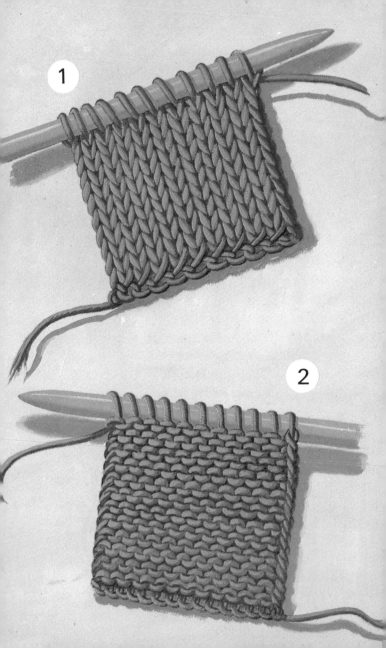

Sewing things together—the overstitch

Some of the things you knit will have to be sewn together, so you must learn how to do this.

First thread some wool into your sewing needle. As this has a large eye, it will be easy to do. With this wool and needle you can join pieces of knitting together.

Pick up two pieces of work you have knitted in stocking stitch. Put these together so that their smooth sides are facing together. Make sure that the two edges to be joined are level with one another.

Keeping the first finger of your left hand between the two pieces of knitting, sew them together. While you are doing this, it helps if you keep your finger near the place where the seam is being stitched. As you make a few stitches, move your finger along. (The picture shows how this is done.)

This is called the OVERSTITCH, and it makes a flat seam.

Something to knit—a pin-cushion for mother

You have already knitted something for yourself—the hair-band. Now you can make something for your mother. Why not make a pin-cushion? This will not take much wool, so find two small balls of different coloured, double knitting wool from your tidy-bag.

Using size 8 needles, cast on 25 stitches with one of the balls of wool. Then knit 30 rows of stocking stitch. When you have done this, cast off the piece of work. You will find that you have made a little square of knitting.

Now make another piece the same way, using the other colour of wool.

When you have made two squares, they must be sewn together. Place the two pieces of knitting together, their smooth surfaces facing one another. Sew *three* of the sides of the squares together, using the overstitch. (If you cannot remember how to make the overstitch, read page 26 again.) Now turn the pin-cushion inside-out, so that the smooth surfaces are outside.

Find some cotton-wool and stuff this inside the pin-cushion. Then sew up the last seam.

You can now give the pin-cushion to your mother.

To make the counting of rows easier, make a mark on a piece of paper each time you finish a row.

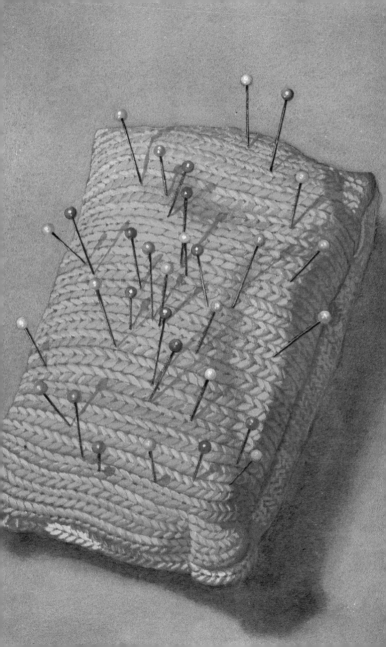

Taking off stitches (decreasing)

Sometimes you will need to reduce the number of stitches on your needle. This is called DECREASING. To do this you make two stitches into one, either at the beginning or the end of a row of plain knitting.

Use the point of the needle you are holding in your right hand to pick up the first two stitches from the needle in your left hand (Picture 1).

Then wind the wool round the needle you are holding in your right hand, just as you did when you were making the plain stitch (Picture 2).

Now pull the loop which you made round the right-hand needle, through the *two* stitches you pushed this needle into. Then slip off both these two stitches from the left-hand needle. You will have knitted two stitches into one (Picture 3).

When you want to take a stitch off (decrease) at the end of a row, you must knit all the stitches along the row in the usual way except for the last two. Then knit these last two stitches together, as explained above.

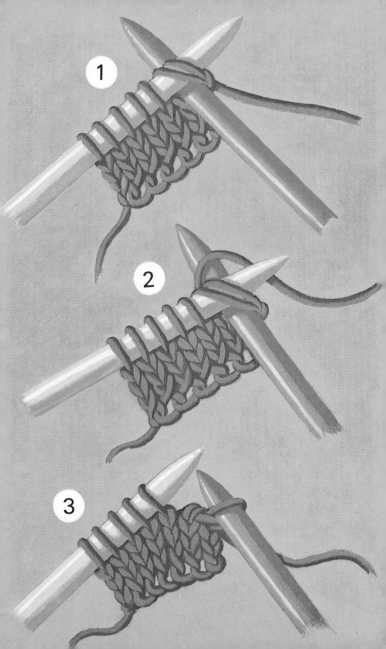

Something to knit—a purse for your pocket money

Now that you have learned how to decrease, you will be able to knit a purse for your pocket money. Any odd ball of double knitting wool will do for this.

Using size 8 needles, cast on 25 stitches. Then knit 50 rows, making garter stitch.

After this you decrease one stitch at the beginning of every row for the next 20 rows. When you have done this, there will be 5 stitches left. Now cast off these 5 stitches.

This piece of work must be sewn up to make it into a purse. Fold over the knitting up to where you started to decrease. Using the overstitch, seam the two sides of the knitting together.

So that you can fasten your purse, sew one half of a press stud under the flap. Then sew the other half of the press stud in the correct position on the outside of the purse. A white button sewn onto the top of the flap will look smart.

When you have made your purse, perhaps your father will give you a bright new one-penny piece to put in it!

Making more stitches (increasing)

You have learned how to take off a stitch (decrease), but sometimes you will have to make *more* stitches.

To do this you have to knit *twice* into the same stitch. This can be done either at the beginning or at the end of a row of plain knitting.

When you want to make an extra stitch, knit the stitch in the usual way, but do NOT slip off this stitch from the left-hand needle (Picture 1). You put the needle held in your right hand through the *back* of this same stitch (Picture 2). Twist the wool round the needle held in your right hand, and knit another stitch. After this, slip off the stitch from the left-hand needle.

When this has been done, you will have made two stitches out of one (Picture 3).

Now carry on knitting the rest of the row in the usual way.

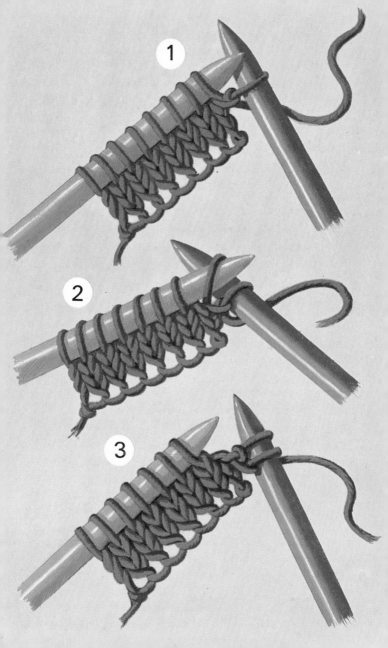

Sewing things together—the back stitch

When you sewed up the pin-cushion you used the overstitch, and this gave a flat seam. However, this is not *always* the best way to sew up pieces of knitting.

Another way is to use the BACK STITCH seam.

Pick up two pieces of knitting and put these together. If they are made in stocking stitch, make sure their right sides are facing each other just as you did when sewing up with the overstitch.

Then with the sewing needle threaded with wool, sew the two pieces of knitting together, making a stitch like a tacking stitch. To make the seam firm, come back over the stitch to 'lock' it. (The picture shows you how to do this.)

This gives a neat, firm seam. You can sew up two pieces of knitting made in garter stitch by using either the overstitch or the back stitch. Because garter stitch looks the same on both sides, it does not matter which sides are together when you sew them up.

Something to make—a ball for a baby

Now that you have learned how to make and take off stitches, you will be able to knit a ball.

To do this you have to make five pieces of knitting all the same size and shape, and using stocking stitch. It is best to find five different colours of double knitting wool for this, as it will make the ball colourful.

Using size 8 needles, cast on two stitches with one of your five colours. Now make a purl row. Then make a plain row BUT at the beginning and end of this row make one extra stitch. This will mean you now have four stitches on your needle. Keep on knitting a row of purl stitches, followed by a row of plain knitting, *making one extra stitch at the beginning and at the end of each plain row* until you have 16 stitches on your needle.

Then knit 12 rows in stocking stitch on these 16 stitches. Follow these with a purl row. Then make a plain row *but decrease one stitch at the beginning and end of this plain row*. This will mean you now have 14 stitches on your needles. Continue knitting a row of purl stitches followed by a row of plain stitches, decreasing one stitch at the beginning and end of each plain row until there are only two stitches left on your needle. Then cast off these two stitches.

You have now made one of the five pieces of knitting, and you must make four more pieces the same way, using other colours.

When you have made the five pieces, sew them together using the overstitch, but leave one seam partly open. Put cotton-wool (or old nylon stockings cut up into small pieces) through this open seam to fill out the ball. Then sew up the last seam.

Making a row of holes in stocking stitch

If you learn how to make a row of holes in stocking stitch knitting, you will be able to thread a piece of ribbon through these and make many interesting things.

When you wish to make a row of holes, you must make them in a row of *plain* knitting.

At the place where you want the hole, bring the wool in front of the needle you are holding in your right hand (Picture 1).

Then put the point of the needle held in your right hand through the next two stitches on the left-hand needle (Picture 2).

These two stitches are then knitted as one in the usual way. On the right-hand needle you now have the loop of wool which you brought forward and the single stitch you made from the two stitches (Picture 3).

Picture 4 shows what a row of holes made every third stitch looks like. You will see how neat the holes are when you have done the next row, which will be purl knitting.

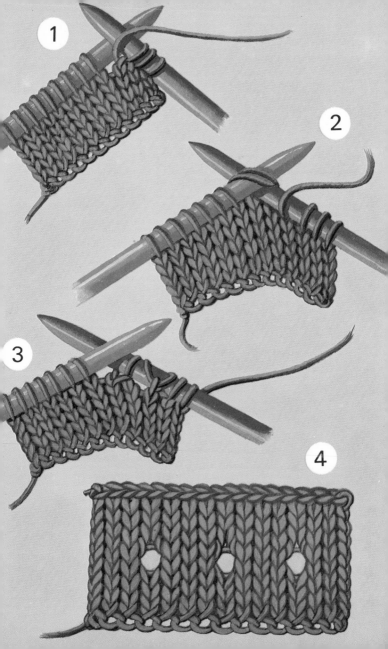

Something to knit—egg-cosies

Now that you know how to make a row of holes, you can make some pretty egg-cosies with ribbon threaded through.

Using size 8 needles and double knitting wool, cast on 28 stitches. Then make two rows in garter stitch. These should be followed by 18 rows in stocking stitch which will bring you to the start of a plain row. After knitting the first stitch of the plain row, make a hole, then knit one stitch, then make another hole—and so on until the end of the row.

When you have finished your row of holes, knit 5 more rows in stocking stitch and then cast off.

Sew up your piece of knitting by folding it round so that the sides meet (smooth surface inside—garter stitch at the bottom). Seam the two sides together, using the overstitch. Turn smooth surface outside, then thread a piece of ribbon through the holes. Draw the ribbon tight and tie a neat bow. Your egg-cosy is now ready for use.

Why not make another one in a different colour, and when you have made two give them as a present to someone.

Something to knit—a blanket for a doll's pram

Now you can knit well, perhaps you would like to make something much larger—say, a blanket for a doll's pram or cot?

You will be able to do this by knitting little squares and sewing them together. You will need lots of odd balls of double knitting wool in bright colours.

Using size 8 needles, cast on 15 stitches with one of your balls of wool. Now knit 22 rows making garter stitch. After these 22 rows, cast off. You will have made a neat little square.

Using different colours of wool, make 14 more squares in the same way as you did the first one. Now you have 15 squares which are all the same size. Lay the squares flat on a table (5 long and 3 wide) to arrange the colours as you would like them.

Sew the squares together using the overstitch. It is best to use white double knitting wool for this, as it will make the blanket look even more attractive.

Then overstitch very neatly all the way round the edge of the blanket to make it look pretty.

Something to knit—a case for your pens and pencils

Why not knit a case in which to keep your pens and pencils? Then you will always know where they are!

You need a ball of double knitting wool for this. With size 8 needles, cast on 50 stitches. Then make 50 rows in stocking stitch. When you have done this, cast off. Then ask your mother to press this well under a damp cloth.

To sew up your case, fold the piece of knitting over so that the smooth surface faces inwards. Then with the back stitch, sew up the two sides of the case but leave the top open.

The knitting is then turned so that the smooth surface of the stocking stitch is on the outside.

Now ask your mother if she can get you a strong zip fastener, long enough to fit the top of the case. Pin this zip into place, tack it and then sew it along the top with back stitch and double, strong cotton. Take care not to get the edge of the knitting too close to the teeth of the zip.

Now your case is ready for your pens and pencils.

Something to knit—a handy bag

Here are the instructions to make something larger—a handy bag.

For this you need a pair of size 8 needles and five good-sized balls of double knitting wool, each in a different colour.

With the size 8 needles, cast on 50 stitches using the green wool. Making stocking stitch knit 6 rows in green, 6 in yellow, 6 in navy, 6 in white, 6 in red, 6 in green, 6 in yellow, 6 in navy and 6 in white.

Now knit 3 rows in the red wool. When making the fourth red row, which should be a knit row, make a row of holes. To do this knit 2 stitches, then bring the wool forward and knit the next 2 stitches together. Then knit 2 more stitches, bring the wool forward and knit the next 2 stitches together. Carry on like this all along the row.

After you have knitted the row of holes, knit 2 more rows in the red wool.

Finally, using the green wool knit 1 row of purl and 5 rows of garter stitch. Then cast off in the green wool.

Make a second piece of work exactly the same as the first one.

Sew three sides of the two pieces of knitting together using the back stitch, leaving the side near the holes open.

To complete your handy bag, plait a cord with the wool you have left over and using this, or a piece of ribbon, thread it through the holes at the top of your bag. This can be pulled tight when you wish to tie up the neck of your bag.

Something to knit—a tie for your father

Why not make a tie for your father in garter stitch?

You will need a full ball of 4 ply knitting wool in a tweed mixture, or perhaps a colour to match your father's clothes.

Using size 9 needles, cast on 14 stitches. Slip the first stitch of the next row onto your right-hand needle without knitting it. Then knit the rest of the row as you have done before.

Slip the first stitch at the beginning of each row without knitting it. This will give your tie a firm edge.

Carry on making the tie until you have about 36 inches of knitting, or measure it against one of your father's ties to be sure it is the correct length.

When your knitting is long enough, cast it off.

You can wrap up the knitted tie you have made and give it to your father as a surprise.